TO ANUROOPIKA, WHO ROARS GENTLY.
—R.S.

TO AMMA, WHO MADE SURE TO RAISE DAUGHTERS
WITH A ROAR INSIDE THEM.
—T.A.

Book design by Melissa Nelson Greenberg & Shriya Jayanthi

Published in 2023 by CAMERON + COMPANY, a division of ABRAMS.

Library of Congress Cataloging-in-Publication Data available.
ISBN: 978-1-951836-84-9

Printed in China

10 9 8 7 6 5 4 3 2 1

CAMERON KIDS is an imprint of CAMERON + COMPANY

CAMERON + COMPANY
Petaluma, California
www.cameronbooks.com

THE LION QUEEN

RASILA VADHER,
THE FIRST WOMAN GUARDIAN
OF THE LAST ASIATIC LIONS

BY RINA SINGH
ILLUSTRATED BY TARA ANAND

cameron kids

"Never look a lion in the eyes,"
my mother warns me before my school field trip to the Gir Forest.
I toss my ribboned braid in the air.
I am not afraid.

Neither is my mother.

The day my father died,
my uncle stomped into the house,
demanding that my sister and I stop
attending school.

"Don't tell me how to raise my children!"
she roared at him.
And he had backed away.

A tiny roar began to grow inside me that day.

My mother never went to school but wanted us to.
She took my father's place at the wheat field
where he had worked for a daily wage.

The only lions I had ever seen were in my schoolbook—
faded yellow and brown.
Now I see them for the first time in flesh and blood.
Like a flash of fire—pure gold.

Here at the Gir Forest, there are many lions.
Once there were thousands.
But for hundreds of years,
the Mughal emperors,
the Indian rajas, and
the British colonists
hunted the lions down until
there were only a few left.

The roar inside me grows.
One day I will take care of the lions.

At home, my mother tries her best to take care of the three of us.
But she can't protect my sister.

Now my once-fierce mother barely raises her voice.
And I don't dare dream about the lions anymore.
Instead, I watch my brother after school,
and together we go to the market to sell peanuts
to pay for our school uniforms and books.

At night I look at the stars—
glinting at me like thousands of lions' eyes.
Night after night, I have only one wish now.
To grow up and take care of my family.

My mother comes running one day.
Gir is hiring forest guards!
My dream come true.

But she wants my brother to try for the job.

I stifle the rumble inside me and go with him.

In the line, he looks at me. I know he's afraid.
I am too.
I know it's a dangerous job.
But suddenly I ask the men if I can try for the job
instead of my brother.
They laugh.
But when they see I won't leave,
they let me, amused.
To their surprise I pass all the tests, and they give me a job—
answering phones and entering rescues in a notebook.
"Why?" I ask.
Because handling wild animals is a man's job.

The roar inside me grows bigger.

I'm the first woman ever to be hired,
and I work hard to prove the men wrong,
working my way from the office to the forest.

When the call comes, I am ready.
Deep in the forest, a lioness is badly hurt.
I offer to capture her so the doctors can take care of her.

For two days, the lioness eludes us.
If I fail, I know I'll never get another chance.

Then I see her. A mother and her cubs.

I aim my dart gun and hit her on the first try.
Slowly she sinks to the ground, sedated.
The doctor quickly treats her wound before she is roused.

I decide the lioness must stay in the forest.
The cubs are too little to survive without their mother.

Two days later, the lioness greets us with a growl;
I know that means she is getting better.

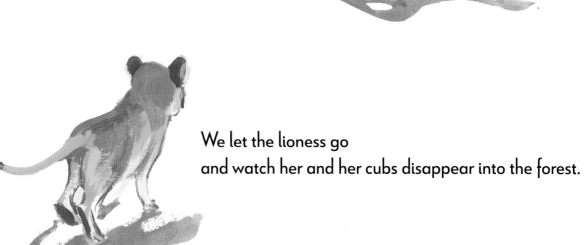

We let the lioness go
and watch her and her cubs disappear into the forest.

Now I lead the rescue team.

When a leopard falls into a deep and dry well, I jump into a cage to rescue the terrified animal.

When a python slithers into the home of a villager, I'm there to capture it in the seething heat, surrounded by a crowd.

When villagers lose their cattle to the hungry lions, I calm them down.

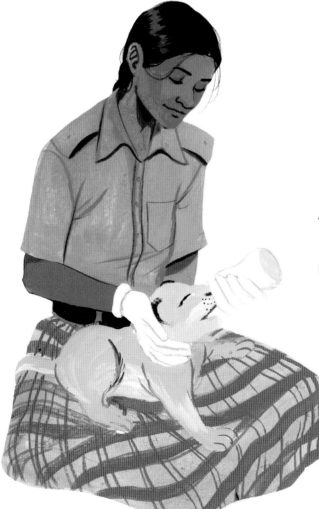

And when it's quiet at the rescue center, I feed the abandoned cubs and hope their mothers will accept them back into their pride.

And when more women join the team,
I take care of them.
I train them to be unafraid of the forest.

At night I roar through the forest on my motorbike
to make sure poachers aren't lurking there.

The forest is full of joy and wonder.
The forest is my home.

One evening, on my last patrol of the day,
I am all alone.

Suddenly, I feel that I'm being followed.
I'm afraid, but I stop and turn my bike around.

And I come face-to-face with the fiercest, most magnificent creature I have ever seen.

Dhak, dhak! Dhak, dhak!
My heart hammers in my chest—
with love. And then fear.
I think of my mother.
But I forget her words.
The lion looks at me, and I look right back at him.

His gaze is fixed—uncertain but powerful.

Hut! Hut! Hut!
I hit my stick on the ground.
I don't look away. He doesn't either.
Then he inches towards me.

I hit the ground again.
He hesitates.
For a long time.
Then he looks away and very slowly,
retreats into the forest.

I ride away,
my heart drumming with excitement.
I looked a lion in the eyes.
I am Rasila—
a Lion Queen.

And I roar.

ABOUT THE LION QUEENS

The Gir National Park in Gujarat, India, is the last known frontier for Asiatic lions in the world. Once a royal hunting ground, Gir is now the only safe place for the lions, also known as Indian lions. First, Mughal emperors hunted the lions. Then, in the 1900s, maharajas and colonial rulers ruthlessly hunted them to near extinction, and their population dwindled to about a dozen. One of the local princes was so alarmed, he banned all hunting. It took a hundred years of conservation to bring the lions back from the brink of extinction. According to the 2020 census, Gir roars with more than six hundred lions. It is one of the most remarkable conservation success stories in the world.

Asiatic lions are still endangered because the sanctuary they live in is becoming too small for their increasing population, and being confined to one location makes them prone to disease and natural disasters.

In 2007, the state of Gujarat hired a handful of women in the department, including the very first: Rasila Vadher. They thought women would opt for safe and easy jobs in the office. But they were wrong. Rasila and her fellow rangers chose to be on the front lines. They formed a rescue team and now save more than six hundred animals a year. Each armed with a walkie-talkie, binoculars, and a stick, these Lion Queens patrol the Gir Forest on foot or on motorbikes, protecting the endangered Asiatic lions. Darting fierce lions with tranquilizers, wrestling with pythons, saving leopards, arresting poachers, nabbing gangs who try to fell and steal teak trees, and nursing abandoned cubs are all in a day's work.

The Lion Queens have created a compassionate environment for the lions, and they have also inspired a whole generation of underprivileged girls who can now dare to dream of working outside their homes for the first time.

Both the lions and women are symbols of beauty and strength, and yet they are so fragile against the forces of man. It's not surprising that the paths of the lions and the Lion Queens crossed and that their stories became intertwined. After all, they both learned to survive against all odds. And survive they did.

ABOUT ASIATIC LIONS

Common name: Asiatic lion

Scientific name: *Panthera leo persica*

Type: mammal

Group name: pride

Average life span in the wild:
    16-18 years

Weight: 300-600 pounds

Diet: carnivorous

- Asiatic lions only live in India.

- Asiatic lions don't look too different from African lions but are much smaller.

- Baby Asiatic lions practice their roar from the time they are born, and by the time they are one year old, the roar is fully developed and is as loud as thunder—and can be heard for miles around them.

ABOUT RASILA VADHER

Rasila Vadher loves the forest and is living her dream, watching over Gir's bounty. When she ventures out, she is always on the lookout for poachers or illegal gangs felling the precious teak trees. She has won the cooperation of the local villagers and the Maldharis, the seminomadic tribal herdsmen who live on the edges of the Gir Forest.

Even though she carries scars from a lion attack in 2012, she is fiercely protective of the lions. She knows no fear. "They are the kings of the jungle and don't bother with humans unless they feel threatened," she says.

A trailblazer, she has been involved in more than 1,100 successful rescue missions and counting. She continues to take care of her family.

SOURCES

The Lion Queens of India,
    Discovery Channel, 2015

Personal interviews with Rasila Vadher

The Story of Asia's Lions, by Divyabhanusinh,
    Marg Publications, India, 2005

When the Last Lion Roars, by Sara Evans,
    Bloomsbury, UK, 2018